C000254747

MABEL LUCIE ATTWELL™
IN CROSS STITCH

'FORGET-ME-NOT' DEAR

MABEL LUCIE ATTWELL™

IN CROSS STITCH

Leslie Norah Hills

GUILD OF MASTER CRAFTSMAN PUBLICATIONS

First published 2005 by
Guild of Master Craftsman Publications Ltd
166 High Street, Lewes
East Sussex, BN7 1XU

Text © Leslie Norah Hills 2005
© in the work GMC Publications Ltd

MABEL LUCIE ATTWELL © Lucie Attwell Ltd. 2005
Licensed by ©opyrights Group

ISBN 1 86108 465 X

All rights reserved

The right of Leslie Norah Hills to be identified as the author of this work has been asserted in
accordance with the Copyright Designs and Patents Act 1988, Sections 77 and 78.

No part of this publication may be reproduced, stored in a retrieval system, or transmitted in any
form or by any means without the prior permission of the publisher and copyright owner.

Whilst every effort has been made to obtain permission from the copyright holders for all
material used in this book, the publishers will be pleased to hear from anyone who has not been
appropriately acknowledged, and to make the correction in future reprints.

This book is sold subject to the condition that all designs are copyright and are not for
commercial reproduction without the written permission of the designer and copyright owner.

The publishers and author can accept no legal responsibility for any consequences arising from
the application of information, advice or instructions given in this publication.

British Cataloguing in Publication Data
A catalogue record of this book is available from the British Library.

Managing Editor: Gerrie Purcell
Production Manager: Hilary MacCallum
Project Editor: Gill Parris

Cover and book design: Maggie Aldred
Photographs: Christine Richardson, back and front cover, styled shots and cross-stitch projects
Mabel Lucie Attwell images: supplied by Copyrights UK
Illustrations: John Yates
Cross-stitch charts: Peter Rhodes

Colour reproduction by CTT Reproduction, London
Printed and bound by Kyodo Printing (Singapore)

For my friend Irene Gannon with thanks
for her help and kindness.

ACKNOWLEDGMENTS

The following books were consulted:

Mabel Lucie Attwell by Chris Beetles and

The Collectable World of Mabel Lucie Attwell by John Henty.

PHOTOCOPYING THE CHARTS

Stitchers may find it helpful to photocopy the charts, so that they can be enlarged for easier use.

Please remember, however, that all the designs are copyright and may not be reproduced commercially without the consent of the designer or copyright owner.

Foreword

Mabel Lucie Attwell's delightful illustrations are as quintessentially English as steam trains and red telephone boxes. Most of us recognize her illustrations, even if we couldn't tell you who the artist was, and like all the best nostalgic things, they just feel comfortably familiar. I first saw her illustrations in my grandmother's collection of *Grimms' Fairy Tales* which I used to read avidly every time we went to stay. I loved the stories but it was the pictures that really fuelled my imagination and gave me so much pleasure.

The appeal of Mabel Lucie Attwell's illustrations spans the generations and I'm delighted to discover I get as much enjoyment from them now as I did then. What I love most is their enduring appeal. Her children seem part of a gentler, more innocent age, and yet they are as mischievous and full of fun as the cheekiest modern child. There's no doubting the personality in every character she's drawn.

Capturing all these little personalities in cross stitch is quite a challenge, but with her artistic eye and extensive design experience, Leslie's done it to perfection. She's faithfully reproduced all the shading and detail without over-complicating the designs, to make them a real joy to stitch. It's going to be a thrill seeing the little characters take shape line by line and watching their faces come alive with the final backstitch details.

The charts in this book have all the ingredients of the most successful cross stitch designs – escapism, nostalgia and that 'feel-good factor' that makes you forget about all those mundane, everyday things and keeps you stitching long into the night with a gentle smile on your face.

Cathy Lewis
Editor, *Cross Stitcher* magazine

Contents

Introduction   10

The Basics   13

Instructions   14

THE DESIGNS

'This one's for <u>you</u>, dear'   23

Layette   27

'Get well quickly!'   33

'The bride, God bless her.

   The bridegroom, God help him'   37

Blowing a kiss   41

Auntie's bathing suit   45

'Just a bundle of love'   49

Sitting by the fire   53

'UR A1 UR!'   57

Girl with dog   61

'They finks I'se going to sleep!'   65

Good luck   69

'Boo-Boo' stationery   73

'As good as his mother ever made!'   79

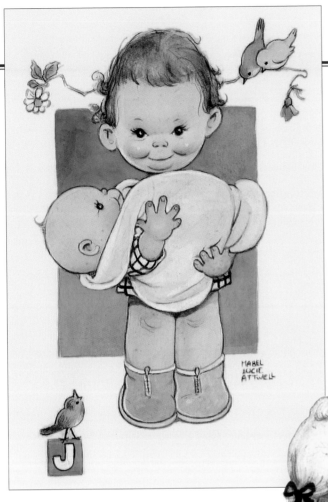

Door plate 113

'White rabbits' 117

Boy with dog 121

Suppliers 124

About the Author 125

Index 126

'Please remember'

   bathroom plaque 83

Secrets 87

'Forget-me-not' 91

Bathroom accessories 95

The fisherman 101

'Puppy' cushion 105

'I likes 'oo!' 109

Introduction

Mabel Lucie Attwell's drawings of chubby babies and young children, which present a nostalgic view of daily life during the inter-war period, have been familiar images for over 50 years and her work is as fresh and as relevant today as it was then.

Mabel Lucie was a very prolific artist and designed more than a thousand postcards at a rate of 24 cards annually. Although her illustrations have been very popular and are now collectors' items, this is the first complete book of cross-stitch designs of her work, many of which are taken from her postcards.

These cross-stitch designs should appeal to all levels of skill: while many of the designs require some experience of cross stitch, there are also simpler designs that will appeal to the less skilled stitcher. The skill level of each design is clearly indicated.

The fabric used throughout is AIDA, mostly in 14 count, although the 'Bathroom Plaque' (pages 82–5) is worked in 16 count. The threads used for the stitched samples are DMC but the equivalent code numbers are given for Anchor threads. There are full working instructions in 'The Basics'.

I have included a short biography of the artist, which runs throughout the book and demonstrates the very full and productive life Mabel Lucie had. In selecting the illustrations for the designs I have chosen those which I felt would be of most appeal to the reader and would be best suited to the technique of cross stitch, but they do not closely follow the biography.

I hope this book will give many hours of pleasure and that you will produce items that will be treasured in the years to come.

Leslie

PAT AND MABEL LUCIE ATTWELL (LATE 1920S)

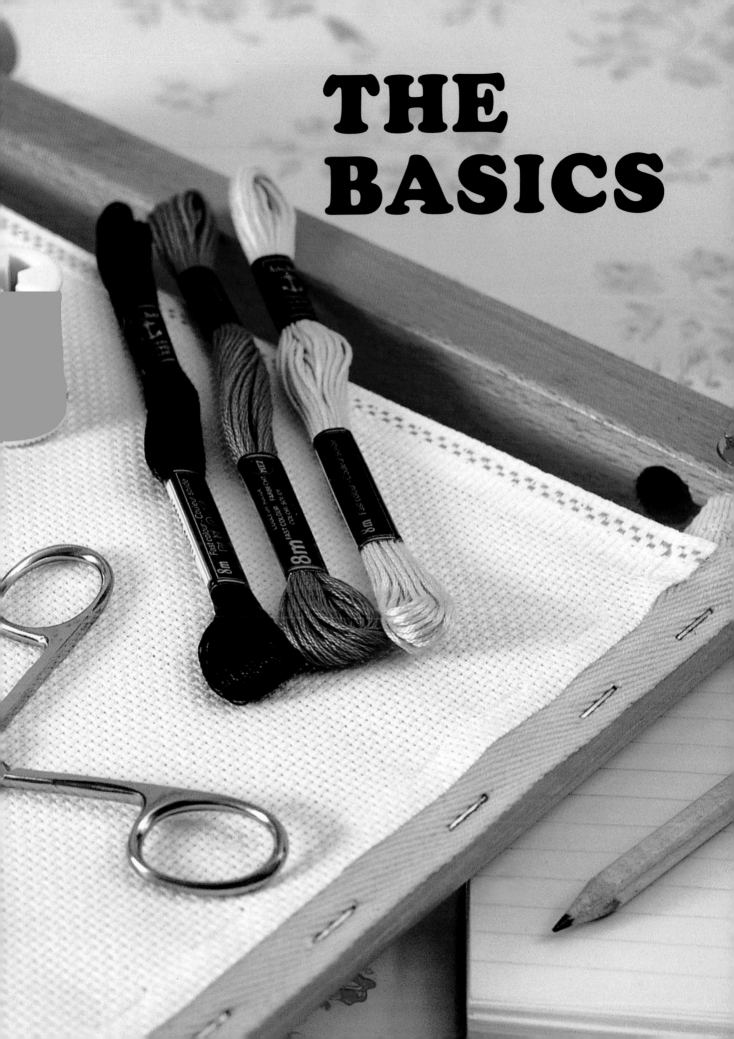

THE BASICS

Instructions

The basic requirements for the designs are very simple. For all of the panels the colour, the fabric and the count is consistent throughout. The threads are also of similar colours in most of the designs. This makes the materials interchangeable and, as a result, reasonably inexpensive.

The stitches used throughout are simple cross stitch, illustrated with charts which include a full list of the materials, together with guidelines on finishing and making up. A colour key for both DMC and Anchor threads is given with each chart.

To work the charts it is quite helpful to have them enlarged and most photocopying services will do this for a small charge. But please remember that even when you enlarge the chart, one square on the chart is still equivalent to one square on the fabric!

Threads

DMC six strand threads are used throughout the book. Each design includes a conversion chart for those readers who prefer to use Anchor alternatives, but the colours may not be exactly as those in the designs.

Two strands of thread are used unless otherwise specified. When using the thread it is advisable to cut the thread into 15in (40cm) lengths, as longer lengths may tangle and become knotted and worn as you use them.

Take care when sewing with metallic thread. It is recommended that you thread your needle in the usual way and use the thread as a double thread. When a metallic thread appears on a sewn section, always sew this after finishing the general sewing.

Needles

Use a tapestry needle for your cross stitch. These are available in several sizes: for general cross stitching a No. 24 size is recommended; for smaller projects use a finer needle as appropriate.

Fabrics

AIDA is the fabric used throughout the book. The count of the fabric determines the finished size of the work you are producing. The higher the count of fabric the smaller the final design. All fabrics have a 'count' and with AIDA this refers to the number of blocks or squares used for working cross stitch. On the charts each 'square' on the chart represents a 'square' on the fabric.

The measurements given for the embroidery fabric include enough to allow for stretching and mounting the finished product. They also allow for binding the edges to prevent them fraying.

Locating Your First Stitch

To determine where to make your first stitch, find the centre of the fabric before you begin. Fold your fabric in half top to bottom, then fold it again from left to right, pinch the centre point and mark it with a pin or thread.

Stitching

CROSS STITCHING

First find the centre of your fabric as instructed above, then find the centre of the chart, which is indicated by the side arrows.

Do not knot your thread! Begin your stitching by inserting your needle from the front of the fabric (1), holding a short length of the thread on the back of the fabric. Work the first few stitches over this length to hold it in place. Work each stitch diagonally from one corner of the 'square' to the opposite corner (2) and then back from the opposite corner again diagonally forming the 'x' (3).

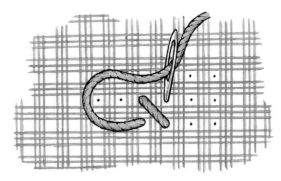

(1)

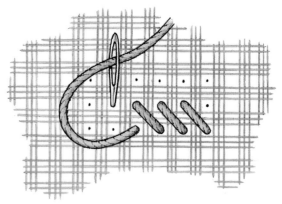

(2)

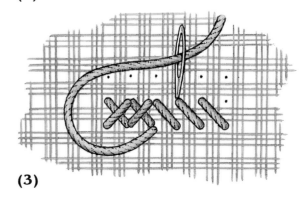

(3)

To ensure the finished cross stitching looks smooth, always work the top threads in the same direction.

HALF CROSS STITCH

This stitch is the first diagonal stitch only and should lie in the same direction as the top stitches of the full cross stitch.

THREE-QUARTER STITCH

Use this stitch when only one half of a graph square is coloured (to form a triangle). Make a half cross stitch, and then bring your needle up through the third hole as if you were going to make a full cross stitch (4). Then pass the needle through the centre of the square over the diagonal half cross stitch (5).

Stitch both colours in the square as full three-quarter stitches. This will ensure an even distribution of colour (6).

BACK STITCH

This stitch is used to outline and define details in the design. The back stitch is indicated by lines drawn onto the charts and the colours used are indicated in the instructions for each chart. Back stitch is a running stitch – two steps forward one step back (7).

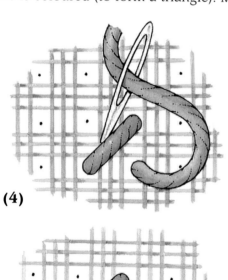

(4)

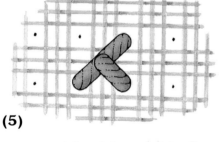

(5)

(6)

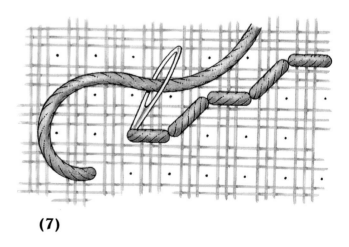

(7)

BLANKET STITCH

Blanket stitch is also called 'buttonhole stitch'. This is formed by making a straight stitch to one side of the previous stitch, with the thread under the needle point, so forming a loop when the stitch is pulled up.

Using a Frame

Larger rectangular frames are more suitable for a larger design (such as the 'Bathroom Plaque', see pages 82–5) and are available in different sizes. Canvas stretchers can be used, provided enough fabric is available. The edges of the fabric are simply tucked under and attached to the frame with drawing pins or staples.

To use a slate frame, cut out the fabric allowing an extra 1–2in (2.5–5cm) turning on the top and bottom edges, and oversew tape to the other two sides. Baste the vertical and horizontal centre lines on the fabric. Working from the centre outwards and using strong thread, oversew the top and bottom edges to the roller tapes (8).

Fit the side pieces of the frame into the slots and roll any extra fabric on one roller until the fabric is taut. Insert the pegs or adjust the screws to secure the frame.

Using a large-eyed needle, secure strong thread around the intersection of the frame. Lace one of the unsecured edges of the fabric to the frame, stretching the fabric evenly. Secure the thread on the intersection at the other end. Repeat to secure the final edge (9).

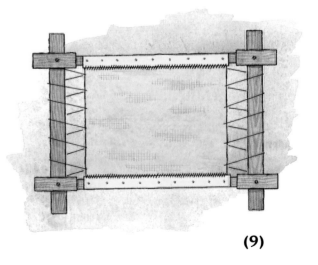

(9)

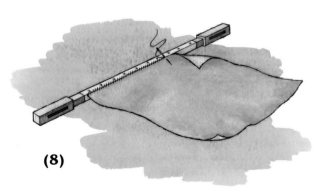

(8)

Using a Hoop

Wooden or plastic hoops – available in different sizes – make popular frames for small designs and are used to hold fabric stretched whilst you stitch. First release the tension screw on the outer ring, centre the fabric over the inner ring and press the outer ring over the top. Gently tighten the tension screw to hold the fabric firmly (10).

(10)

Solving Potential Problems

KNOTS

Sometimes, as you work, you will find that your thread develops a knot. When this happens, don't panic. It can usually be undone by sliding your needle into one of the loops of the knot and easing it loose by gently pulling the ends of the thread to straighten it.

UNPICKING

If the worst happens and you need to unpick a part of your work it is easier than you may think. First look at the chart you are working from carefully and compare it with the fabric to see where you have gone wrong. Use sharp, pointed scissors and snip the top diagonal stitch to be removed, then use your needle to pull out the stitches carefully one by one.

It is advisable to work in the order that the stitches were first put in. If you cannot remember this, snip the top half of one or two more stitches before trying again. When you have removed the stitches use your needle to pull the thread ends to the wrong side of the work. Then secure these under the other stitches as you begin to work again.

Washing Your Work

If you would like to wash the finished work, use lukewarm water with a gentle fabric detergent. Rinse thoroughly, place between the folds of a clean towel and gently press the excess water out.

Allow the work to dry naturally, then pad your ironing board with a clean towel and place your work face down on top. Position a clean tea towel over the work and press with a warm iron using a circular movement.

Mounting Embroidery

It is advisable to ask a professional framer to mount your embroidery, but if you wish you can do this for yourself.

First cut a piece of cardboard to the size of the finished design with an extra allowance so that it will fit snugly in the recess in the frame. Place the work face down and centre the card on top. Fold over the top and bottom edges of the fabric and lace them together across the back of the card using a strong thread (button thread is good for this). Repeat on the other two sides, mitring the corners,

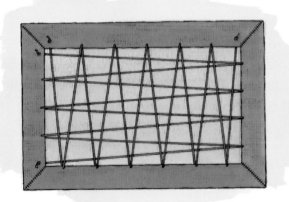

(11)

and pull up the lacings tightly to stretch the fabric over the card (11). Overstitch the mitred corners to neaten them and check that the design is centred at the front.

Finally, place in a frame of your choice and enjoy!

Mitring Corners

• To mitre cushion corners, sew the border strips onto the embroidered fabric. Fold one border strip over the other, making sure it is lying at right angles to the other, and pin in place.

• Draw a straight line on the strip at a 45˚ angle from the inner corner to the edge. Change over the fabric strips and draw another line at a 45˚ angle. These two lines indicate the sewing line.

• With right sides together, match the lines and pin, and then sew the strips together.

• Repeat for the other three corners and trim. Press your work.

• With right sides together, sew the backing fabric to the front on three sides.

• Finally, put in the cushion pad and hand stitch the base closed.

THE DESIGNS

'This one's for you, dear'

MABEL LUCIE ATTWELL WAS BORN 4TH JUNE 1879 IN THE EAST END OF LONDON, ENGLAND, THE NINTH CHILD OF AUGUSTUS AND EMILY ATTWELL. HER FATHER WAS A BUTCHER WHO WORKED LOCALLY, AND THE VERY HAPPY HOUSEHOLD IN WHICH THE FAMILY LIVED PROVIDED MABEL LUCIE WITH THE INSPIRATION TO SKETCH PICTURES OF FAMILIES AND BABIES.

THIS ONE'S FOR YOU DEAR.

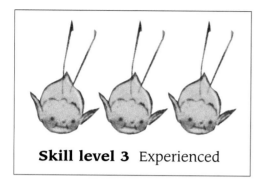

Skill level 3 Experienced

THIS ONE'S FOR YOU, DEAR

'This one's for you, dear'

		DMC	ANCHOR
	Dark red	321	9046
	Red	606	335
	Orange	722	323
	Yellow	725	305
	Light yellow	727	293
	Dark yellow ochre	833	907
	Yellow ochre	834	874
	Light brown	3828	943
	Light orange	3827	363
	Green	470	267
	Light green	3817	875
	White	blanc	2
	Grey	3024	397
	Black	310	403

NOTES

Use 14 count AIDA fabric
in cream
Use two threads for the
cross stitch
Use one thread for the
back stitch

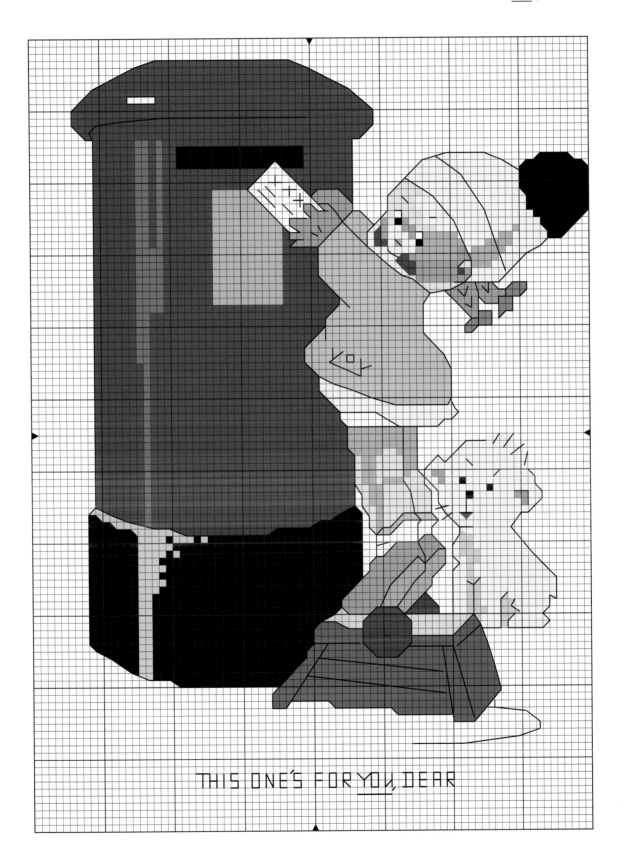

Layette

MABEL LUCIE SOLD HER FIRST ILLUSTRATION IN 1894, WHEN SHE WAS 15. LATER SHE RECOUNTED THAT HER FAMILY, ESPECIALLY HER BROTHERS WHO WERE BECOMING BRILLIANT MUSICIANS, THOUGHT SHE WAS COMPLETELY MAD TO WANT TO BE AN ARTIST. WHEN SHE TOOK TWO PICTURES TO A PUBLISHER BECAUSE SHE WANTED TO EARN SOME POCKET MONEY, HER BROTHERS JEERED AND SAID SHE WAS MAKING A SILLY FOOL OF HERSELF. BUT, A FEW DAYS LATER, SHE RECEIVED AN ENVELOPE CONTAINING A CHEQUE FOR TWO GUINEAS — £2.10 (US$3.75) IN TODAY'S CURRENCY, BUT A PRINCELY SUM IN THOSE DAYS.

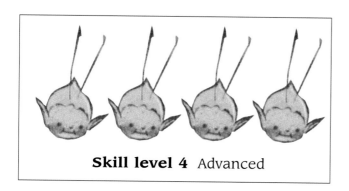

Skill level 4 Advanced

Stitching the Vest

• Tack a piece of waste canvas 3 x 3in (8 x 8cm) onto the area you wish to embroider and mark with a pin where you want the centre of the design to be (see 'Locating Your First Stitch', on page 15).

• Work the cross stitches in the usual way, using two strands of thread. It helps to use a sharper needle on this fabric (No. 28 is recommended) but it is not imperative. It is really important, however, to make sure that the points of all the cross stitches touch each other neatly.

• When the stitching is complete, take out the tacking stitches and trim the waste canvas to about 1in (2.5cm) around the embroidery.

• Using a small sponge or tissue, moisten the waste canvas threads all over until they become limp.

• Then, using a pair of tweezers, gently pull out the waste canvas threads one by one, so as not to distort the stitching. They should come out quite easily if you remove the threads that run in one direction first, and then those that run in the other direction.

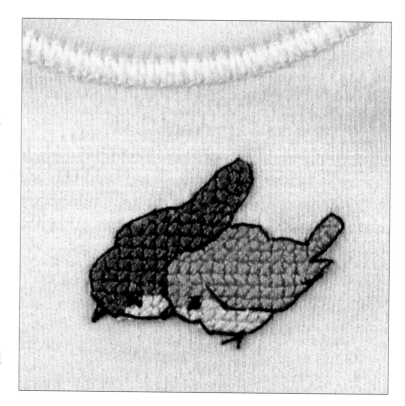

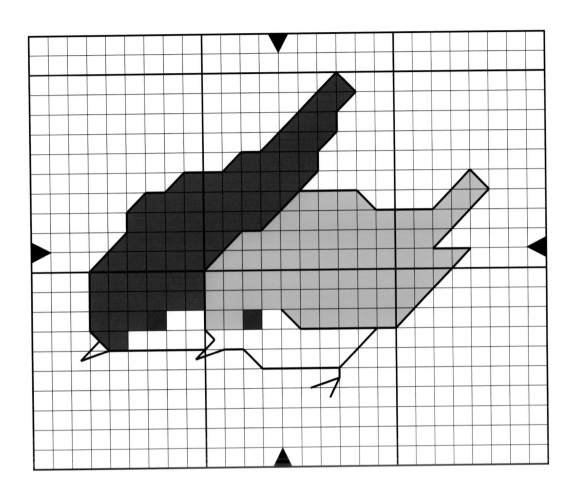

Baby vest

		DMC	ANCHOR
■	Blue	3807	122
▨	Yellow	3820	306
■	Brown	838	380
☐	White	Blanc	2
■	Black	310	403

NOTES

Use baby vest with
waste canvas
Use two threads for the
cross stitch
Use one thread for the
backstitch in black

Bootees

• The area for stitching on the front of the bootees is so small that it is immediately apparent where the design has to go. Work with two strands of embroidery thread in your needle for all the stitching and begin working from the central point of the chart.

• Work each cross stitch across one square of the fabric, ensuring that the upper strands of each stitch follow the same direction to give a neat effect.

• Refer to the chart and key constantly to complete the cross stitching, and remember that each square of the chart represents one stitch.

NOTES

Use DMC bootees in 14 count AIDA

Use two threads for the cross stitch

Use one thread for the back stitch in black

Bootees

		DMC	ANCHOR
■	Dark red	815	43
■	Light brown	420	374
■	Dark brown	300	352
□	Cream	Ecru	387
■	Black	310	403

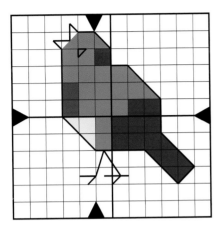

Rattle

Follow the same instructions as
for the bootees.

Rattle

		DMC	ANCHOR
	Dark red	815	43
	Light brown	420	374
	Dark brown	300	352
	Cream	Ecru	387
	Black	310	403

NOTES

Use DMC rattle with
14 count AIDA bib
Use two threads for
the cross stitch
Use one thread for the
back stitch in black

GET WELL QUICKLY!

'Get well quickly!'

FROM 1895–1900 MABEL LUCIE ATTENDED A PRIVATE SCHOOL AND LATER STUDIED AT ST MARTIN'S SCHOOL OF ART IN LONDON. IT WAS THERE THAT SHE MET HER FUTURE HUSBAND, HAROLD EARNSHAW, WHO WAS SEVEN YEARS HER JUNIOR. MABEL LUCIE DID NOT ENJOY THE CLASSICAL TEACHING AT ST MARTIN'S, BUT IT GAVE HER A BASIC GROUNDING IN DESIGN. SHE WAS PLEASED WHEN LATER SHE LEFT AND BEGAN WORK FOR THE BOOK PUBLISHERS W & R CHAMBERS, AS AN ILLUSTRATOR.

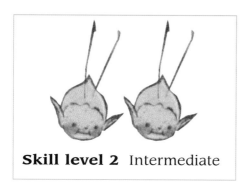

Skill level 2 Intermediate

'Get well quickly!'

		DMC	ANCHOR
	Pale pink	3770	1009
	Mid pink	353	6
	Dark pink	352	9
	Dark brown	838	380
	Yellow	3821	305
	Green	520	862
	Red	666	46
	Dark blue	3807	122
	Light blue	809	130
	Black	310	403
	White	Blanc	2

NOTES

Use 14 count AIDA fabric
in white
Use two threads for the
cross stitch
Use one thread for the
back stitch in black

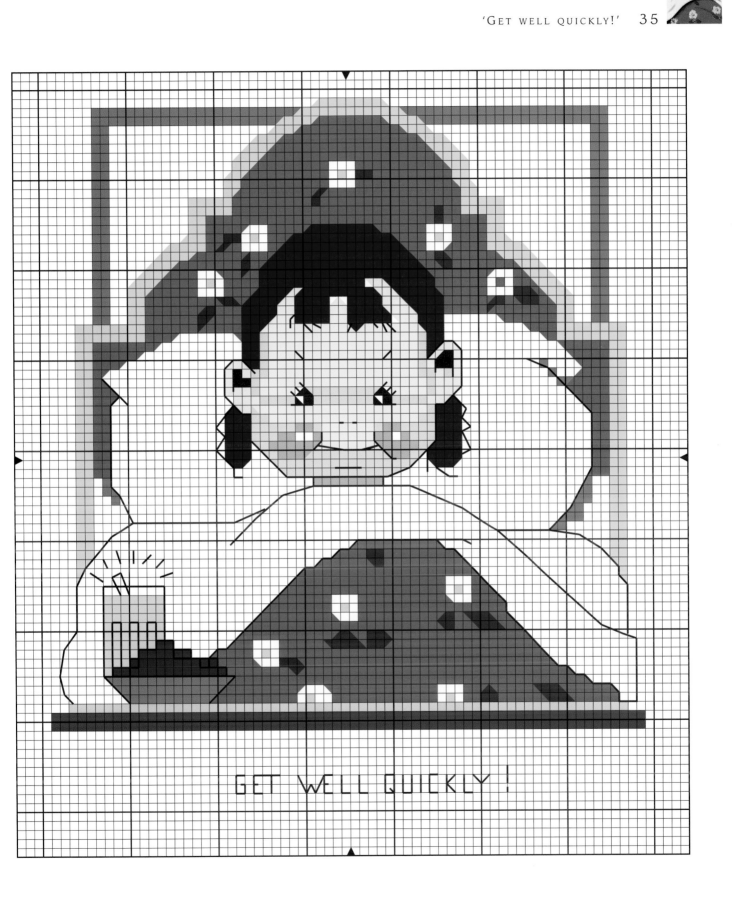

'The bride, God bless her. The bridegroom God help him'

MABEL LUCIE AND HAROLD EARNSHAW, WHOM SHE CALLED 'PAT', MARRIED IN A REGISTRY OFFICE IN 1908, ON MABEL LUCIE'S 29TH BIRTHDAY. ALTHOUGH PAT'S SISTER KITTY AND MABEL LUCIE'S BROTHER NORMAN ATTENDED, THE ABSENCE OF HER PARENTS SUGGESTS THAT IT WAS WITHOUT THEIR APPROVAL. OUTSIDE A BARREL ORGAN WAS PLAYING THE TUNE 'WHEN WE ARE MARRIED'.

THE BRIDE, GOD BLESS HER. THE BRIDEGROOM GOD HELP HIM

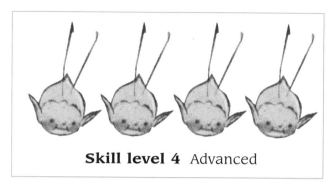

Skill level 4 Advanced

NOTES

Use 14 count AIDA fabric
in white

Use two threads for the
cross stitch

Use one thread for the
back stitch

All in black except dark pink
for the roses and white on
the jacket and shoes

'The bride, God bless her. The bridegroom, God help him'

		DMC	ANCHOR
	White	Blanc	2
	Ecru	Ecru	387
	Grey	647	1040
	Pale pink	3770	1009
	Dark pink	950	4146
	Pale orange	3824	9475
	Dark orange	351	10
	Dark brown	838	380
	Light brown	3790	393
	Beige	644	830
	Light green	470	267
	Dark green	702	226
	Light blue/green	3817	875
	Yellow ochre	3821	305
	Black	310	403

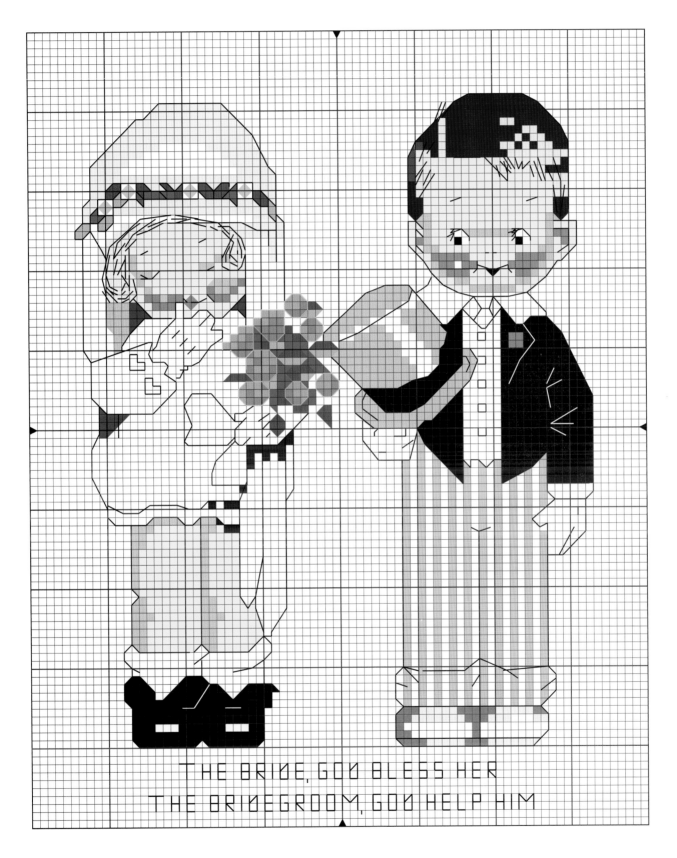

THE BRIDE, GOD BLESS HER
THE BRIDEGROOM, GOD HELP HIM

Blowing a kiss

IN 1909, WHILST MABEL LUCIE AND HER HUSBAND WERE LIVING IN A MODEST FLAT IN LONDON, PEGGY, THEIR FIRST BABY, WAS BORN. A MYTH HAS DEVELOPED THAT PEGGY WAS THE INSPIRATION FOR MABEL LUCIE'S TODDLERS, BUT THIS WAS DISMISSED BY MABEL LUCIE, WHO IS QUOTED AS SAYING: 'I NEVER FOUND INSPIRATION IN WATCHING MY CHILDREN. THEY JUST LIVED UP TO THE IDEAS I HAD ALREADY BEEN DRAWING FOR YEARS.'

I'SE JUST BLOWING A KISS
TO A DEAR THAT I MISS!

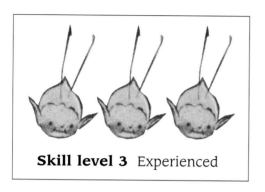

Skill level 3 Experienced

Blowing a kiss

		DMC	ANCHOR
⬛	Blue	809	130
⬜	Cream	Ecru	387
⬜	Pale pink	819	271
⬜	Pink	3713	1020
⬜	Mid pink	776	24
⬜	Dark pink	760	1022
⬜	Yellow	725	305
⬛	Light brown	781	309
⬛	Brown	838	380
⬛	Black	310	403
☐	White	Blanc	2

NOTES

Use 14 count AIDA fabric in white

Use two threads for the cross stitch

Use one thread for the back stitch in black except the crosses on her dress, which are in blue

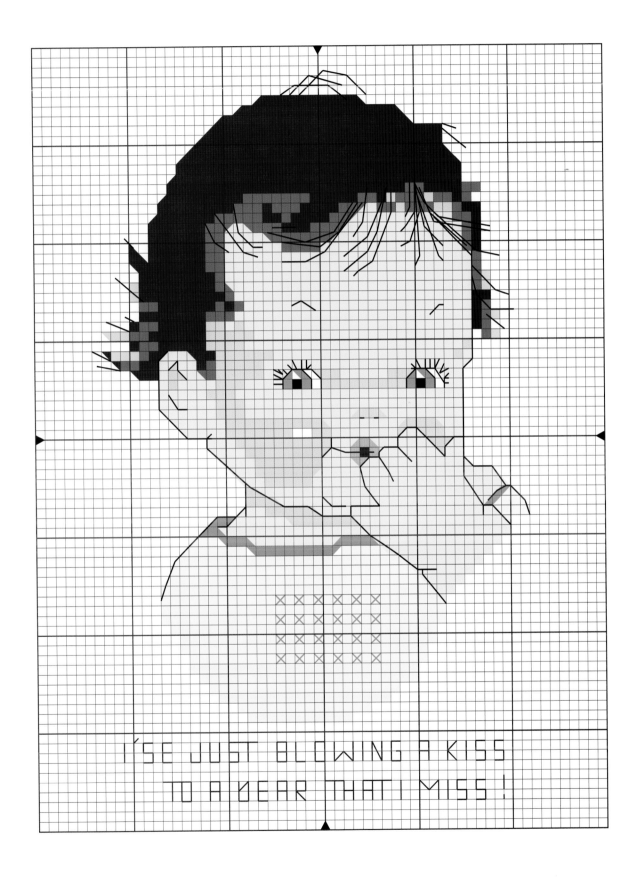

Auntie's bathing suit

MABEL LUCIE QUICKLY BECAME WELL KNOWN TO COMMERCIAL FIRMS AS THEY DISCOVERED THE APPEAL OF HER ILLUSTRATIONS, SUCH AS THIS ONE. LONDON UNDERGROUND COMMISSIONED A SERIES OF POSTERS FROM HER, ONE OF WHICH 'HULLO, DID YOU COME BY UNDERGROUND?', SOLD IN UNPRECEDENTED NUMBERS.

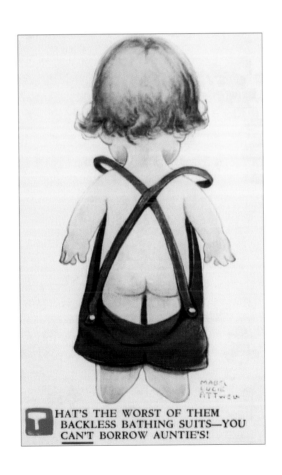

HAT'S THE WORST OF THEM BACKLESS BATHING SUITS—YOU CAN'T BORROW AUNTIE'S!

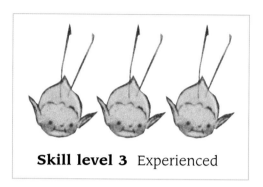

Skill level 3 Experienced

NOTES

Use 14 count AIDA fabric
in white
Use two threads for the
cross stitch
Use one thread for the
back stitch in dark brown

Auntie's bathing suit

		DMC	ANCHOR
	Pale pink	948	1011
	Pink	945	881
	Turquoise	3810	168
	Green	561	212
	Yellow	676	891
	Brown	300	352
	Dark brown	838	380

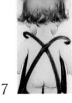

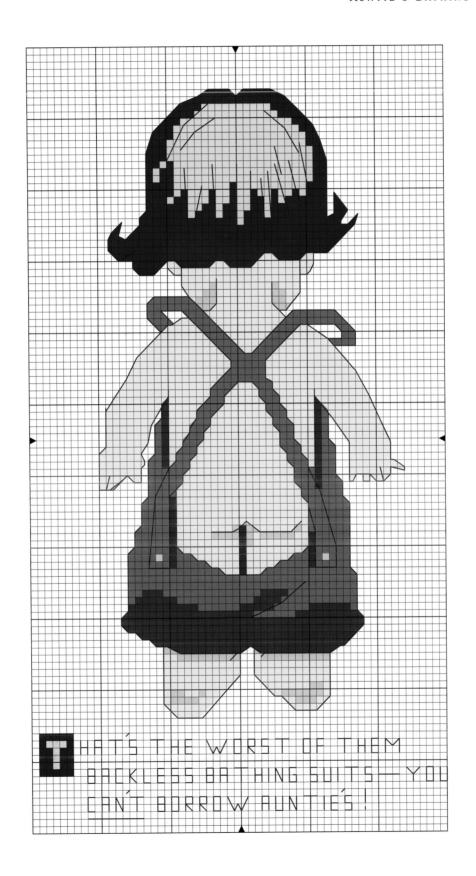

THAT'S THE WORST OF THEM
BACKLESS BATHING SUITS—YOU
CAN'T BORROW AUNTIE'S!

'Just a bundle of love'

M ABEL LUCIE AND PAT'S FIRST BABY WAS BORN IN 1909. SHE WAS NAMED MARJORIE, BUT CALLED 'PEGGY'. MABEL LUCIE LATER SAID: '... MOTHERHOOD WAS THE MOST WONDERFUL THING IN MY LIFE. MY CAREER IS ME, AND MY PICTURES ARE ME, BUT NO WRITER OR SCIENTIST COULD MAKE ANYTHING AS PERFECT AS A BABY, AND YET THROUGH ME IT HAS BEEN DONE.' BETWEEN 1910 AND 1917 MABEL LUCIE ILLUSTRATED SIX VOLUMES FOR THE *RAPHAEL HOUSE LIBRARY OF GIFT BOOKS.*

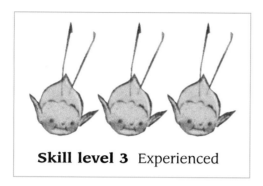

Skill level 3 Experienced

NOTES

Use 14 count AIDA fabric in white

Use two threads for the cross stitch

Use one thread for the back stitch and lettering in dark brown

'Just a bundle of love'

		DMC	ANCHOR
	Pale pink	819	271
	Mid pink	225	1026
	Dark pink	224	893
	White	Blanc	2
	Dark brown	838	380
	Blue	799	136
	Yellow	745	300
	Salmon pink	353	6
	Brown	301	1049

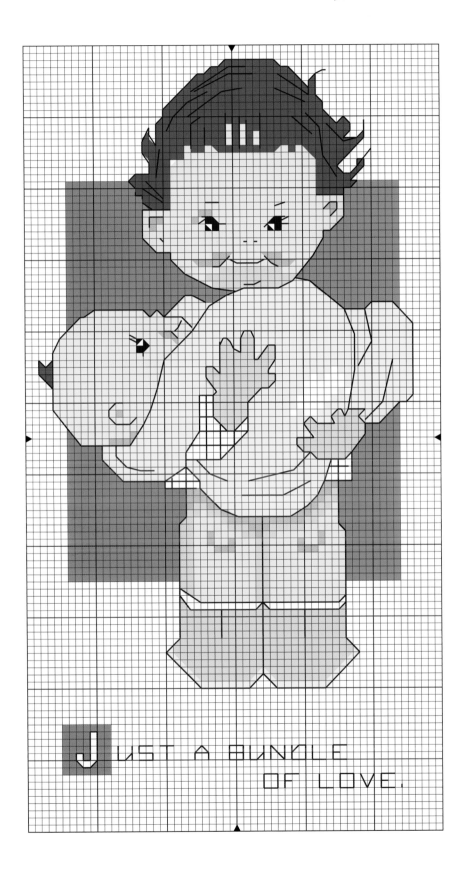

Sitting by the fire

IN 1911 Mabel Lucie's first son, Max, was born. The parents later renamed him 'Peter' or 'Pete' as the First World War was looming and the name 'Max' was felt to be too Germanic and unpatriotic. They were living in a cottage-style house in Surrey, south-east England, close to the Farthing Downs. Later that year the family moved to a larger house in the same district, and created a large studio out of two bedrooms.

Skill level 1 Beginners

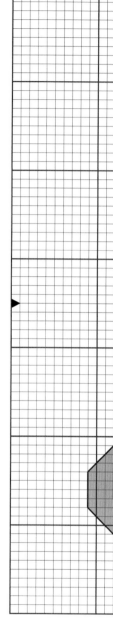

Sitting by the fire

		DMC	ANCHOR
	Sugar pink	3609	85
	Blue	340	118
	Red	3687	68
	Cream	3770	1009
	Pink	818	23
	Russet	436	1045
	Brown	3064	884
	Green	959	186
	Grey	415	398
	Dark brown	838	380
	White	Blanc	2

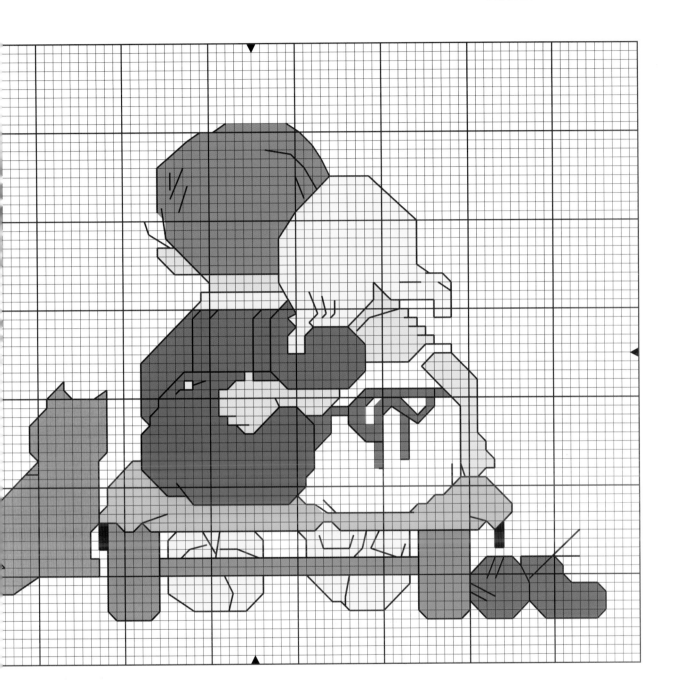

NOTES

Use 14 count AIDA fabric in white. Use two threads for the

cross stitch and one thread for the back stitch in dark brown

'UR A1 UR!'

Later in 1911, Mabel Lucie began her long association with the postcard manufacturers Valentine & Sons of Dundee. She produced a huge quantity of designs for postcards, greetings cards, calendars, shopping lists, booklets, jigsaw puzzles and plaques. These continued to the end of her working life. Many of her postcards contributed greatly to the war effort and were used as a means of recruitment and propaganda.

"U.R. 'A.1.'—U.R.!"

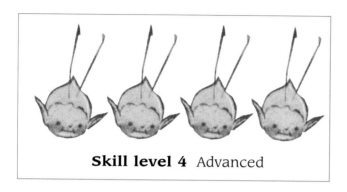

Skill level 4 Advanced

'UR A1 UR!'

NOTES

Use 14 count AIDA fabric
in white
Use two threads for the
cross stitch
Use one thread for the
back stitch

'UR A1 UR!'

		DMC	ANCHOR
■	Very dark pink	351	10
■	Dark pink	352	9
■	Medium pink	3824	9475
■	Pink	950	4146
■	Pale pink	3770	1009
■	Green	3817	875
■	Dark blue	796	133
■	Red	606	335
■	Cream	Ecru	387
■	Yellow	727	293
■	Brown	3790	393
■	Grey	647	1040
■	Light grey	644	830
■	Black	310	403
□	White	Blanc	2
■	Yellow ochre	3821	305

UR-"A1"-UR

Girl with dog

IN 1915 MABEL LUCIE ATTWELL'S HUSBAND JOINED THE ARTISTS' RIFLES AND ENTERED THE FIRST WORLD WAR. HE WENT TO THE FRONT ON THE SOMME IN FRANCE AND DURING A BATTLE IN 1916 HE LOST HIS RIGHT ARM. AFTER THE INJURY HE SAID: 'I REMEMBER SITTING UP AND THINKING I WAS LUCKY TO BE ALIVE AND I HAD, EVEN THEN, VISIONS OF A NICE CLEAN BED IN HOSPITAL AND A VISIT TO BLIGHTY.' IT WAS A POTENTIAL DISASTER FOR A MAN WHO EARNED HIS LIVING AS AN ARTIST, BUT HE SHOWED GREAT DETERMINATION AND BEGAN TO DRAW USING HIS LEFT HAND. HIS HEALTH WAS NEVER GOOD AFTER THIS INJURY.

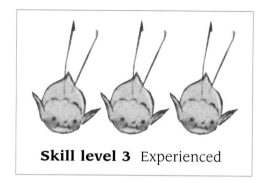

Skill level 3 Experienced

Girl with dog

		DMC	ANCHOR
	Mid pink	776	24
	Pale pink	819	271
	Pink	3713	1020
	Dark pink	760	1022
	Yellow	445	288
	Green	987	244
	Brown	838	380
	White	Blanc	2
	Black	310	403
	Red	309	42
	Ecru	Ecru	387

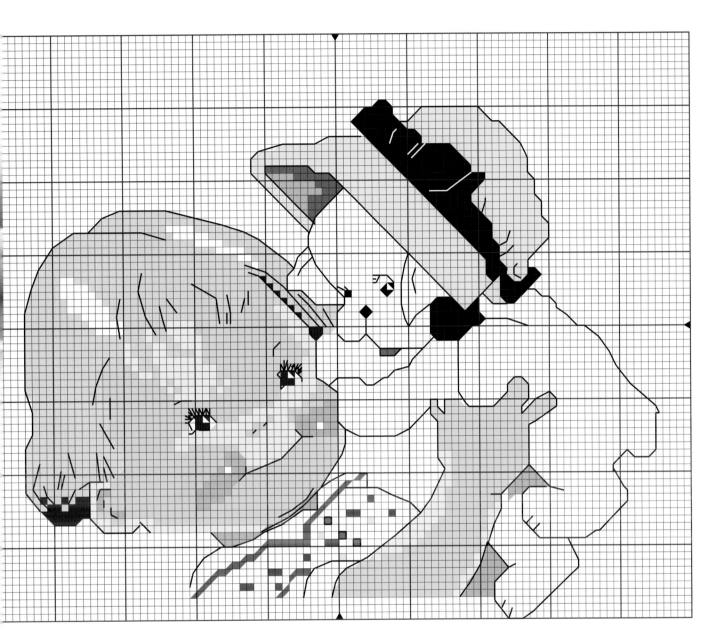

NOTES

Use 14 count AIDA fabric in white

Use two threads for the cross stitch

Use one thread for the back stitch in black

White back stitch on bonnet ribbon

'They finks I'se going to sleep!'

MABEL LUCIE'S DEFINITION OF THE 'BABY TALK' CAPTIONS SHE APPLIED TO HER DRAWINGS WAS A CONTRIVED ADULT VIEW OF CHILDHOOD. SHE LATER EXPLAINED TO CHARLES HAMBLETT OF THE *DAILY SKETCH* NEWSPAPER: 'I SEE THE CHILD IN THE ADULT, THEN I DRAW THE ADULT AS A CHILD. THE SITUATION, THE STANCE AND THE VOCABULARY ARE TAKEN FROM CHILDREN, BUT THE MESSAGE IS BETWEEN ADULTS.' IN 1914 HER SECOND SON, BRIAN (CALLED 'BILL'), WAS BORN.

THEY FINKS I'SE GOING TO SLEEP!

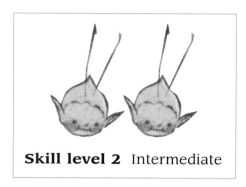

Skill level 2   Intermediate

'They finks I'se going to sleep'

		DMC	ANCHOR
	Dark pink/orange	352	9
	Light pink/orange	353	6
	Cream	3770	1009
	Blue	809	130
	White	Blanc	2
	Lavender	211	342
	Pink	3354	74
	Ecru	Ecru	387
	Brown	3790	393
	Light blue	3753	1031

NOTES

Use 14 count AIDA fabric
in white
Use two threads for the
cross stitch
Use one thread for the
back stitch in brown

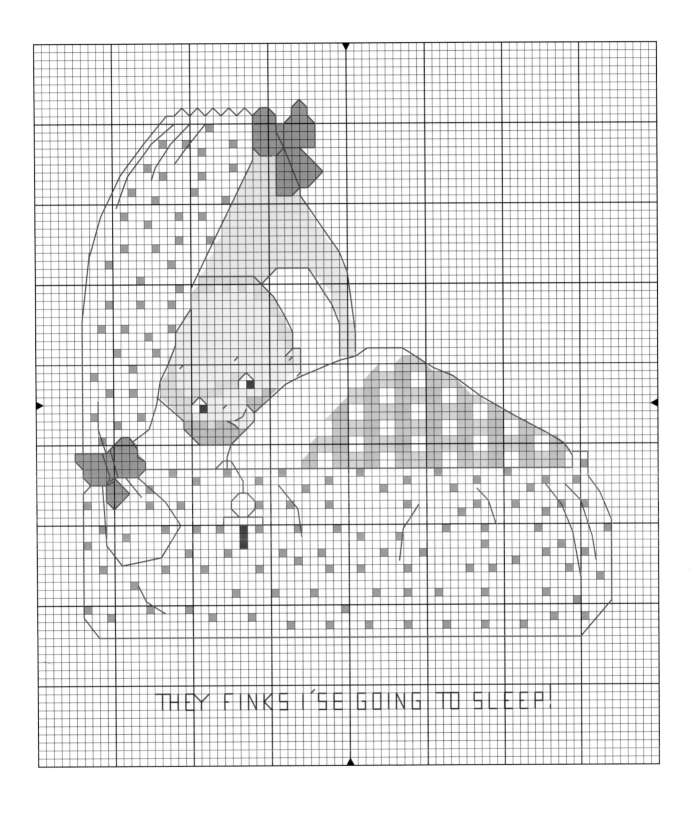

Good luck

In 1919 Mabel Lucie's publishers asked her to design eight illustrations for *Peeping Pansy*, a book written by the Queen of Romania. Mabel Lucie became friends with the queen and was invited to stay at the royal palace so that they could work more closely together. The queen told Mabel Lucie that she kept a copy of her books of illustrations near her 'As a comfort for when I am in the dumps'.

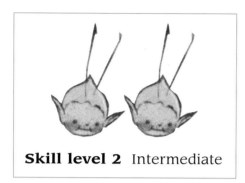

Skill level 2 Intermediate

Good luck

		DMC	ANCHOR
	Pale pink	3713	1020
	Pink	776	24
	Dark pink	760	1022
	Light yellow	445	288
	Yellow	307	289
	Light cerise	603	62
	Dark cerise	3350	65
	Blue	796	133
	Black	310	403
	White	Blanc	2
	Silver thread		

NOTES
Use 14 count AIDA fabric
in white
Use two threads for the
cross stitch
Use one thread for the
back stitch

'Boo-Boo' stationery

IN 1920 THE FAMOUS 'BOO-BOOS' WERE CREATED. THESE FUNNY LITTLE ELVES, WHO WERE ALWAYS DRESSED IN GREEN, WERE EXTREMELY POPULAR WITH CHILDREN. AS A CONSEQUENCE THEY WERE INCLUDED IN SIX STORYBOOKS AS A SERIES OF FAIRY TALES, WERE SUBSEQUENTLY MADE INTO SOFT TOYS, AND ALSO USED AS ILLUSTRATIONS ON NURSERY TEA SERVICES.

I'SE JUST ARRIVED

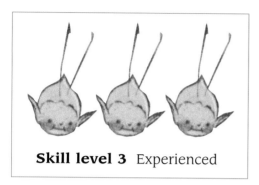

Skill level 3 Experienced

Note Block

The note block has a space between the outside clear plastic and the inner liner. Between these you insert your embroidery.

• Using the inner lining as a template, carefully draw in pencil around the plastic lining onto the 22 count Hardanger. Use this as a guide for your work.

• After the cross stitch has been completed, wash your work as described in 'The Basics', on page 18, and insert into the note block together with the inner lining.

• Fill with the sheets of paper provided and your note block is ready for use.

Note block

Note block

		DMC	ANCHOR
⬛	Green	989	242
⬛	Brown	3790	393
⬜	Pale pink	225	1026
⬜	Pink	760	1022
⬛	Lavender	340	118
⬜	Yellow	744	301

Notes

Use 14 count AIDA fabric in white

Use two threads for the cross stitch

Use one thread for the back stitch in brown

Bookmark

• Cut a piece of 22 count Hardanger fabric to size 10 x 8in (25 x 20cm).

• Follow the chart and complete the embroidery.

• Fold the bookmark into three sections with the embroidery in the centre. Allow a border at the upright edges of ⅜in (1cm). Fray down the top and bottom sections to the stitched border.

• Neatly stitch the back together allowing a small hem. Catch together the top and bottom section with white thread between the frayed section. Lightly press and your bookmark is ready for use.

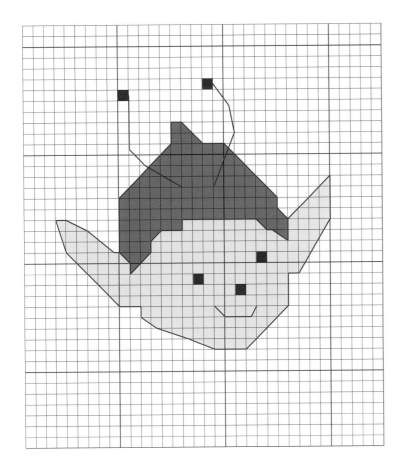

Label

Work the embroidery on 22 count Hardanger.

• Trim the finished work to 2in (5cm). And carefully fray the edges.

• Buy a gift bag and attach the label to the side using a white paper glue.

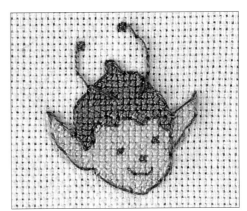

Bookmark and label

		DMC	ANCHOR
■	Green	989	242
■	Brown	3790	393
□	Pale pink	225	1026
▨	Pink	760	1022
■	Lavender	340	118
□	Yellow	744	301

'As good as his mother ever made!'

In 1922 Mabel Lucie was invited to visit the Queen of Romania. She had never travelled abroad before and her agent offered to accompany her on the visit. After she arrived safely in Romania, he returned to London. Mabel Lucie wrote in a letter home: '...poor shy, little me. Pitched right into the very middle of a royal family, ceremony and trappings complete.'

"As good as his mother ever made!"

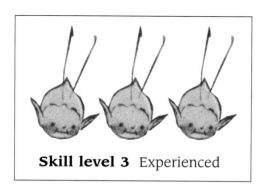

Skill level 3 Experienced

'AS GOOD AS HIS MOTHER EVER MADE!'

'As good as his mother ever made!'

		DMC	ANCHOR
■	Rust	355	1041
■	Creamy yellow	727	293
■	Yellow	445	288
■	Bright yellow	307	289
■	Green	470	267
■	Dark blue	796	133
□	White	Blanc	2
■	Black	310	403
■	Brown	3790	393
■	Cream	Ecru	387
■	Dark cream	677	886
■	Yellow ochre	676	891
■	Rust pink	352	9
■	Dark rust pink	351	10

NOTES

Use 14 count AIDA fabric in white

Use two threads for the cross stitch

Use one thread for the back stitch

Back stitch on apron in 355

All other back stitch in 310

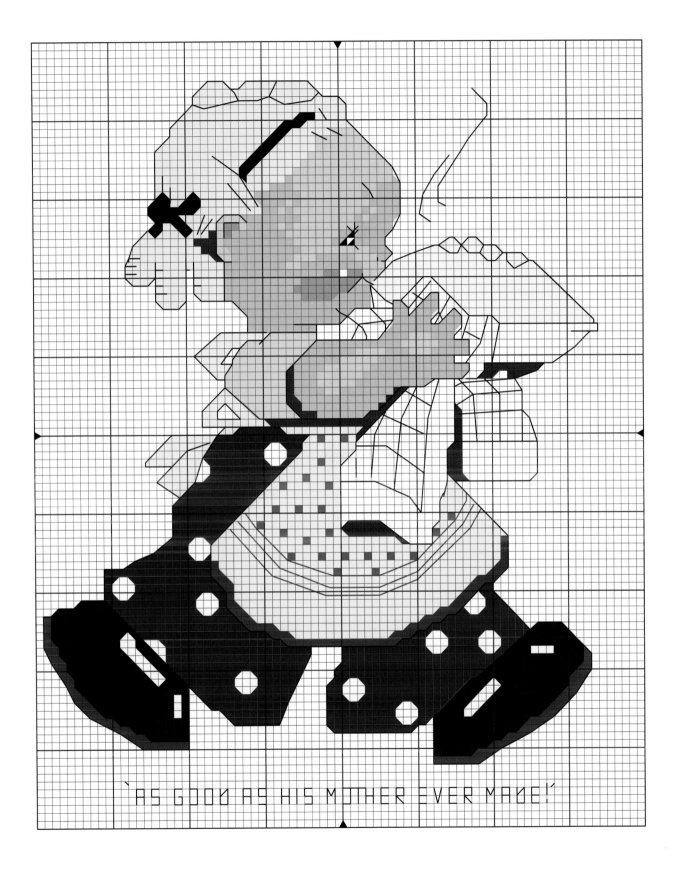

'AS GOOD AS HIS MOTHER EVER MADE!'

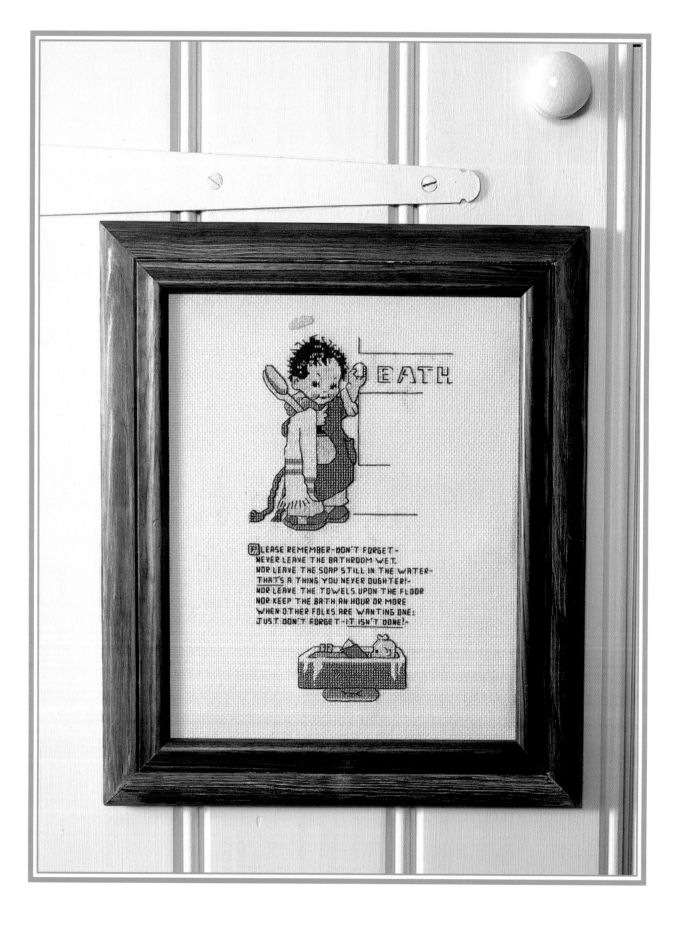

'Please remember'
bathroom plaque

THE 'PLEASE REMEMBER – DON'T FORGET' DESIGN BECAME THE MOST POPULAR OF MABEL LUCIE ATTWELL'S IMAGES. IT WAS PRODUCED IN 1929 AS A BATHROOM PLAQUE AND HAS SOLD AS SUCH IN HUNDREDS OF THOUSANDS. PEOPLE FROM ALL WALKS OF LIFE BOUGHT IT, AND IT HAS BECOME A LASTING ICON TO HER WORK.

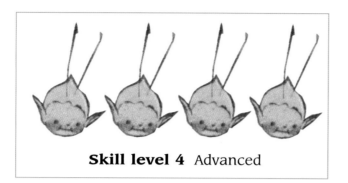

Skill level 4 Advanced

To Mount the Bathroom Plaque

Follow the instructions for 'Mounting Embroidery', on page 19 of 'The Basics'.

'Please remember'

		DMC	ANCHOR
	Pale pink	819	271
	Mid pink	818	23
	Dark pink	224	893
	White	Blanc	2
	Pale green	747	158
	Green	564	206
	Blue	932	1033
	Yellow	745	300
	Cream	Ecru	387
	Blue/purple	340	118
	Orange	3776	1048
	Brown	436	1045
	Dark brown	838	380

NOTES

Use 14 count AIDA fabric
in Sky 550
Use two threads for the
cross stitch
Use one thread for the
back stitch
Use dark brown thread
for the long stitch and the
lettering

Secrets

I N 1930 MABEL LUCIE'S DAUGHTER PEGGY WAS MARRIED TO MICHAEL WICKHAM, BUT THEIR MARRIAGE ONLY LASTED EIGHT YEARS. THEY HAD TWO CHILDREN, THE ONLY GRANDCHILDREN THAT WERE BORN TO MABEL LUCIE AND PAT. DURING THIS TIME THE EARNSHAWS RENTED A FARMHOUSE IN THE CUCKMERE VALLEY, EAST SUSSEX, A BEAUTIFUL AREA OF SOUTHERN ENGLAND, AND SPENT AS MUCH FREE TIME AS THEY COULD THERE. THEY LIKED THE AREA SO MUCH THAT THEY LATER BOUGHT A HOUSE THERE.

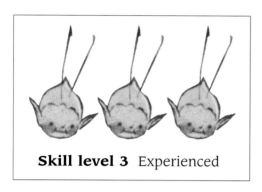

Skill level 3 Experienced

NOTES

Use 14 count AIDA fabric
in white

Use two threads for the
cross stitch

Use one thread for the
back stitch in dark brown

Secrets

		DMC	ANCHOR
	Pale pink	819	271
	Pink	3713	1020
	Mid pink	776	24
	Dark pink	760	1022
	Blue	809	130
	Red	309	42
	Beige	950	4146
	Cream	712	926
	Mid beige	407	914
	Brown	838	380
	Dark beige	3772	1007
	White	Blanc	2
	Black	310	403

'FORGET-ME-NOT' BEAR

'Forget-me-not'

PAT'S HEALTH BEGAN TO FAIL IN 1934 AND IN 1935 THEIR SON BRIAN DIED SUDDENLY OF PNEUMONIA AGED 20. SO THIS WAS A VERY SAD TIME FOR MABEL LUCIE. HOWEVER, SHE CONCENTRATED ON CARING FOR HER HUSBAND AND NURSING HIM THROUGH HIS FINAL ILLNESS, AND STILL MANAGED TO PRODUCE A SMALL NUMBER OF POSTERS AND NEW POSTCARDS DURING THIS PERIOD.

"FORGET-ME-NOT." DEAR.

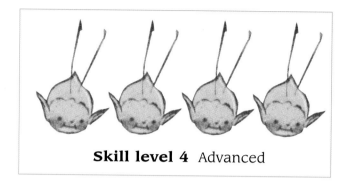

Skill level 4 Advanced

'Forget-me-not'

		DMC	ANCHOR
	Yellow	3821	305
	Orange	977	1002
	Rust	301	1049
	Blue	519	1038
	Green	470	267
	Yellow ochre	834	874
	Brown	838	380
	Black	310	403
	Cream	Ecru	387
	Mid cream	739	366
	Dark cream	738	361
	Salmon pink	352	9
	Dark salmon pink	351	10
	White	Blanc	2
	Dark rust	918	341

'FORGET-ME-NOT' DEAR

NOTES

Use 14 count AIDA
fabric in white
Use two threads
for the cross stitch
Use one thread for
the back stitch
Back stitch on hair:
Dark rust
Back stitch on beads:
301
Back stitch on flower
stems: Green
Back stitch on
lettering: Black

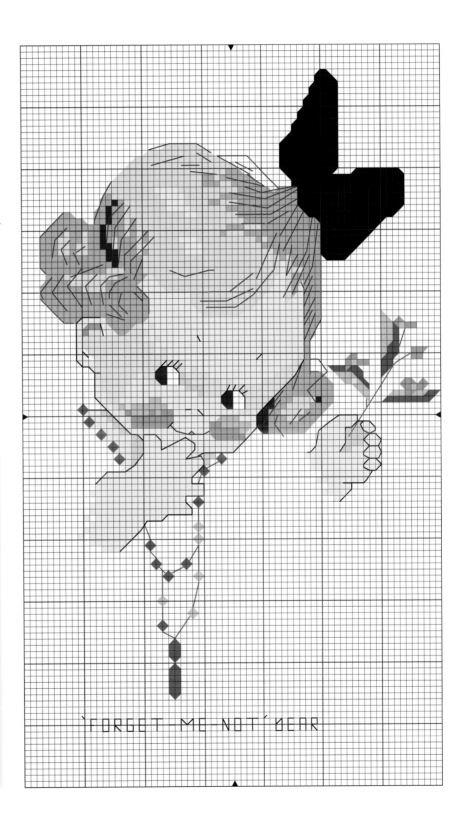

Bathroom accessories

I N 1935, BECAUSE OF PAT'S ILL HEALTH, MABEL LUCIE AND HER HUSBAND MOVED BACK TO LONDON, TO A SMALL TERRACED HOUSE IN KENSINGTON. HER DAUGHTER PEGGY RECALLED IN 1970: 'IN SPITE OF PRODUCING A FORMIDABLE BODY OF WORK, SHE FOUND TIME TO RUN A HAPPY HOME. IN FACT, LOTS OF THEM AS SHE WAS A GREAT ONE FOR MOVING. THIS CERTAINLY GAVE HER AMPLE OPPORTUNITIES TO INDULGE HER TALENT FOR MAKING RELAXED, AND ELEGANT INTERIORS.'

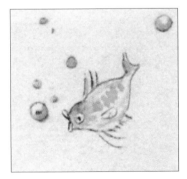

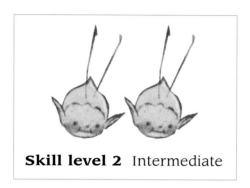

Skill level 2 Intermediate

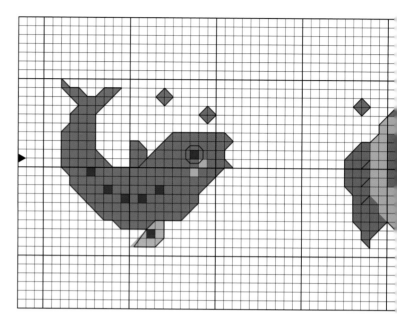

Hand towel

Hand towel

		DMC	ANCHOR
	Lime green	3819	278
	Light green	959	186
	Mid green	991	189
	Dark green	934	862

NOTES

Use 14 count AIDA plastic
fabric in white

Use two threads for the
cross stitch

Use one thread for the
back stitch in dark green

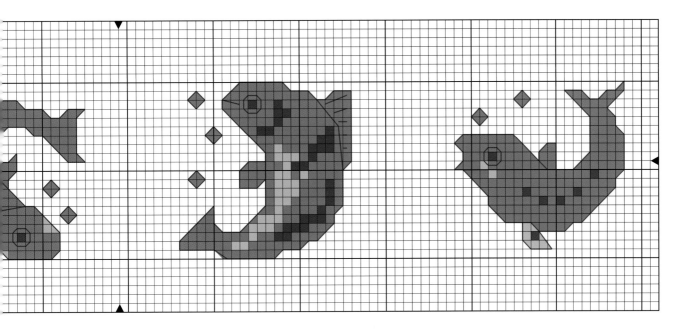

Hand Towel

• Fold the AIDA band on the
towel in half lengthwise to find
the centre. Mark this with a pin
or thread.

• Begin stitching the fish,
working the position by counting
the squares from the centre.
Use two threads for the
cross stitches and one thread
for the back stitch.

• When the stitching is complete,
hand wash the towel carefully
in warm water, as instructed on
page 18. Lay it face down on a
towel and allow to dry.

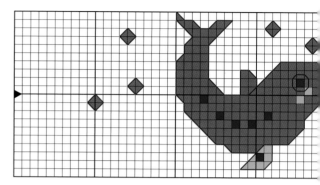

Soap dispenser

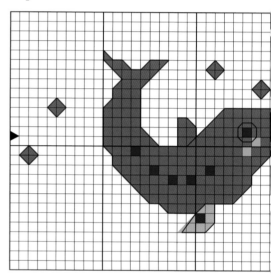

Tooth mug

Soap Dispenser and Tooth Mug

These items can be obtained from Meineck Design Group – see 'Suppliers', on page 124, for details.

• Inside the kit you will find a strip of plastic 14 count fabric. Fold this in half horizontally to find the centre. Mark this with a small piece of thread and count to the first fish. Use two threads for the cross stitching and one thread for the back stitch.

• When the stitching is complete remove the inner section of the tooth mug or soap dispenser and place the plastic fabric with your stitching on into the unit.

• Replace the inner section and screw on the top.

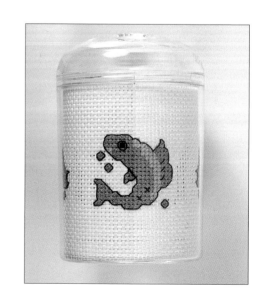

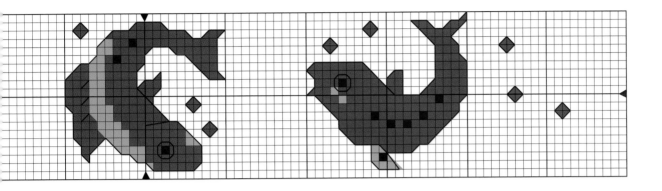

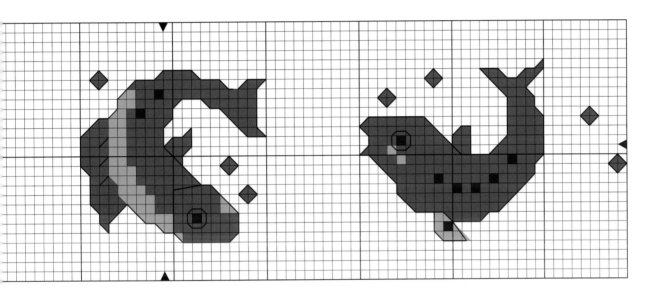

Soap dispenser and tooth mug

		DMC	ANCHOR
	Lime green	3819	278
	Light green	959	186
	Mid green	991	189
	Dark green	934	862

The fisherman

Mabel Lucie's husband died on 17th March 1937. He was buried by the side of their son Brian, near to their former home in the Cuckmere Valley. His headstone reads, 'In memory of Harold Cecil Earnshaw who died of war wounds on March 17th 1937, aged 51 years'.

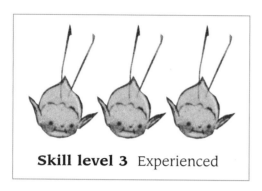

Skill level 3 Experienced

NOTES

Use 14 count AIDA fabric
in white
Use two threads for the
cross stitch
Use one thread for the
back stitch in dark brown

The fisherman

		DMC	ANCHOR
	Pale pink	819	271
	Pink	3354	74
	Brown	3772	1007
	Beige	950	4146
	Yellow	727	293
	Orange	783	307
	Green	959	186
	Cream	Ecru	387
	Dark brown	838	380
	Dark green	3812	188
	White	Blanc	2
	Pale green	3756	1037

'Puppy' cushion

After the death of her husband Mabel Lucie moved to a pretty stucco house in Kensington, London, an area she had always favoured. She was restless, however, and found it hard to settle after the sadness of her family misfortunes. Within a year she moved to another house nearby, and then to a hotel, followed by a move to another house, this time in North London.

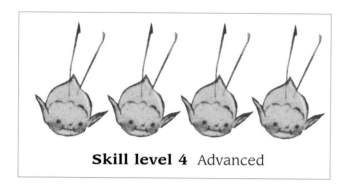

Skill level 4 Advanced

Making up the Cushion

Fabric required: approximately 39in (1m) of blue fabric – preferably spotted.

Cushion pad 17 x 17in (43 x 43cm).

* Cut a square of fabric 18 x 18in (45 x 45cm) for the back of the cushion and set aside.
* Cut four strips of fabric from the remaining fabric 4 x 19in (10 x 48cm).
* Trim finished embroidery to 12 x 12in (30 x 30cm).
* Working with one strip at a time and with the rights sides together, pin the first strip to the top of the embroidery allowing ¾in

Embroidering the Cushion

* Use Zweigart 14 count AIDA in sky blue 12 x 12in (30 x 30cm).
* Stitch with two threads throughout and use brown thread for the outlines and detail.

'Puppy' Cushion

		DMC	ANCHOR
☐	White	blanc	2
☐	Yellow	727	293
■	Red	347	1025
■	Black	310	403
■	Beige	3064	883
■	Brown	838	380

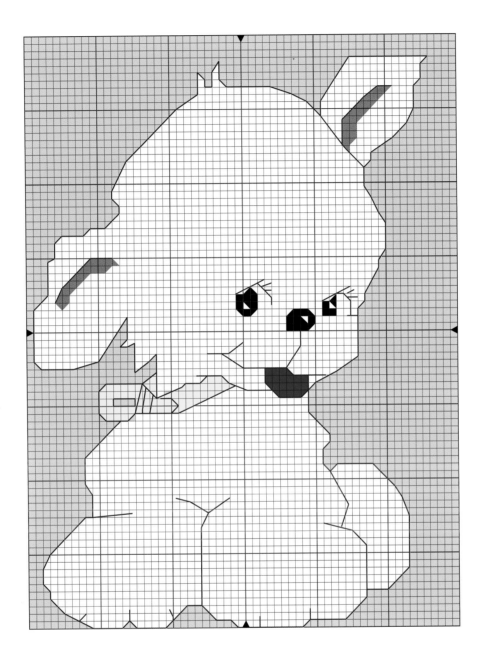

(2cm) along the design edge. Ensure it is centrally placed and then sew it in position. To allow for the mitred corners, do not sew right to the edges only to the side margin.

• Sew on the bottom strip and then the side strips.

• To complete the cushion, mitre the corners, following the instructions given in 'The Basics', on page 19.

'I likes 'oo!'

Patronage was extended to Mabel Lucie by members of the royal household, including Princess Elizabeth, the future Queen, and her sister Princess Margaret, who ordered a Christmas card from Mabel Lucie in 1937 called 'There are Fairies' and, in the following year, another entitled 'Christmas Eve'. The Queen, then Princess Elizabeth, used Mabel Lucie's designs in the royal nurseries and Prince Charles owned a set of china decorated with her designs.

I LIKES 'OO!

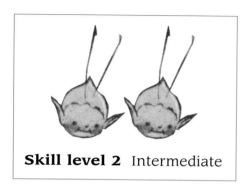

Skill level 2 Intermediate

'I likes 'oo!'

		DMC	ANCHOR
	Cream	Ecru	387
	Pale pink	948	1011
	Pink	945	881
	Dark pink	407	914
	Yellow	744	301
	Pale green	3819	278
	Green	470	267
	Light brown	436	1047
	White	Blanc	2
	Brown	300	352
	Black	310	403

NOTES

Use 14 count AIDA fabric
in white

Use two threads for the
cross stitch

Use one thread for the
back stitch in brown

Door plate

BETWEEN 1937 AND 1940 MABEL LUCIE MOVED HOUSE SEVERAL TIMES WITHIN WEST LONDON. WITH THE OUTBREAK OF WAR IN 1939 SHE WAS BUSY PRODUCING MORALE-BOOSTING POSTCARDS AND CONTRIBUTED TO THE *QUEEN'S BOOK OF THE RED CROSS*. AT THE HEIGHT OF THE BLITZ IN 1940 SHE STAYED WITH HER DAUGHTER IN WILTSHIRE, SOUTHERN ENGLAND, AND SUBSEQUENTLY MOVED IN WITH HER WHEN SHE FOUND HER FINAL LONDON HOUSE WAS TOO SMALL TO ACCOMMODATE THE FAMILY PIANO.

LITTLE SISTER —
NEW FROM HEAVEN.

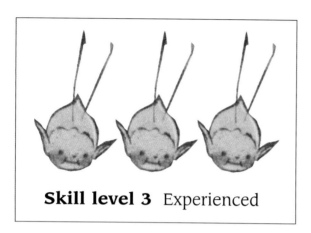

Skill level 3 Experienced

Door plate

		DMC	ANCHOR
	Lavender	340	118
	Green	988	243
	Red	321	9046
	Blue	825	162
	Cream	945	881
	Yellow	744	301
	Brown	301	1049
	Pink	3609	85
	White	Blanc	2

NOTES

Use 14 count AIDA fabric
in white

Use two threads for the
cross stitch

Use one thread for the
back stitch

Outline the pink ribbon
in red

Outline everything else
in brown

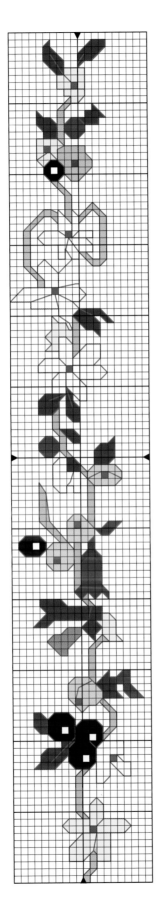

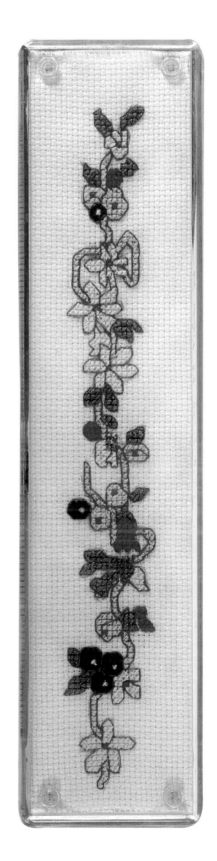

'White rabbits'

In 1943 Mabel Lucie moved to Cornwall, south-west England, and moved again two years later to her final home in that area. Her explanation for this move was given in an article in *Homes and Gardens* magazine in 1961: 'While I was in Cornwall I was lucky enough to hear of a house for sale — the sale to include a telephone. I did not particularly want the house, but I did want the telephone. I got both. It may be a prosaic thing to be the deciding factor and my reason for living in Cornwall, but it is a true one.'

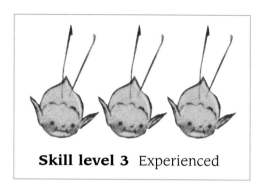

Skill level 3 Experienced

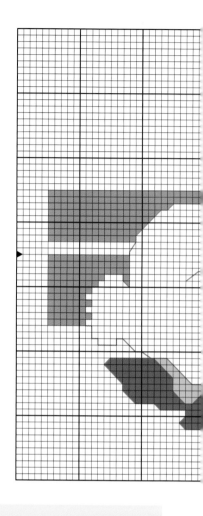

'White Rabbits'

		DMC	ANCHOR
☐	White	blanc	2
	Pink	225	1026
	Orange	722	323
	Pale green	472	253
	Green	989	242
	Dark green	561	212
	Black	310	403
	Grey	451	233

NOTES

Use 14 count AIDA fabric
in white

Use two threads for the
cross stitch

Use one thread for the
back stitch in grey

For the eyes put one small
stitch of white to highlight
the eye

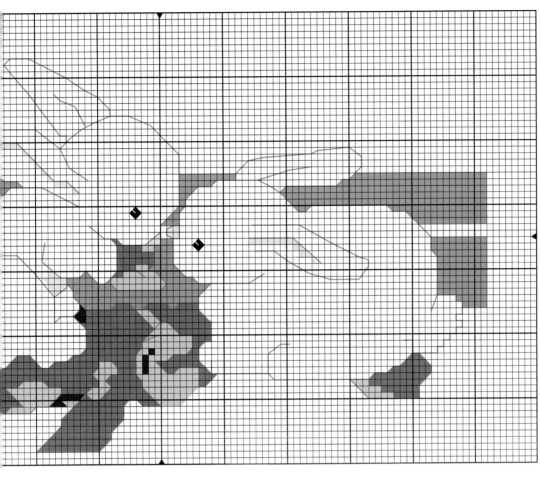

Boy with dog

MABEL LUCIE ATTWELL DIED ON 5TH NOVEMBER 1964, AGED 85. SHORTLY BEFORE SHE DIED SHE SAID: 'MY LIFE HAS BEEN GOOD AND SAD. I HAVE, ACCORDING TO MANY LETTERS I HAVE RECEIVED, GIVEN A LOT OF HAPPINESS TO A LOT OF PEOPLE THROUGH TWO WORLD WARS.' HER DAUGHTER PEGGY SUMMED UP HER MOTHER'S SUCCESS: 'MOTHER JUST DID WHAT SHE WANTED TO DO AND THAT WAS WHAT THE PUBLIC LIKED. AND THEN SHE HAD THE DRIVE AND APPLICATION TO GO ON AND ON PRODUCING IT.'

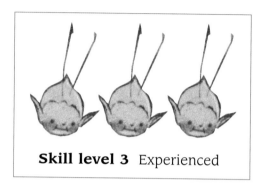

Skill level 3 Experienced

NOTES

Use 14 count AIDA fabric
in white

Use two threads for the
cross stitch

Use one thread for the
back stitch in black

Boy with dog

		DMC	ANCHOR
	Pale pink	819	271
	Pink	818	23
	Dark pink	224	893
	Blue	340	118
	Green	3816	876
	Grey	3024	397
	White	Blanc	2
	Cream	Ecru	387
	Yellow	738	361
	Brown	301	1049
	Black	310	403

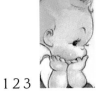

Suppliers

DMC

UK

DMC Creative World Ltd
62 Pullman Road
Wigston
Leicester LE8 2DY
Tel: + 44 (0) 116 281 1040

USA

The DMC Corporation
Port Kearny Building
10 South Kearny
NJ 07032
Tel: + 1 (0) 973 344 0299

AUSTRALIA

DMC Needlecraft Pty Ltd
PO Box 317
Earlwood
NSW 2206
Tel: + 61 (0) 2 95593088

COATS
(Anchor Threads)

UK

Coats Crafts UK
PO Box 22
McMullen Road
Darlington
Co. Durham DL1 1YQ
Tel: + 44 (0) 1325 394 394

USA

Coats North America
4135 South Stream Blvd
Charlotte
North Carolina 28217
Tel: + 1 (0) 704 329 5800

AUSTRALIA

Coats Paton Crafts
Level 1
382 Wellington Road
Milgrave
Victoria 3170
Tel: + 61 (0) 39561 2288

FABRICS

Willow Fabrics
95 Town Lane
Mobberley
Knutsford WA16 7HH
Tel: + 44 (0) 08000 567 811
www.willowfabric.com

ACCESSORIES

Meineck Design Group
Hendraburnick Farmhouse
Davidstow
Camelford
Cornwall PL32 9SG
Tel: 01840 261270
Fax: 01840 261528
www.meineck.com
Email: MDG@btinternet.com

Framecraft Ltd
372–376 Summer Lane
Hockley
Birmingham
England B19 3QA
Tel:+ 44 (0) 121 212 0551

About the Author

Leslie Norah Hills comes from an artistic background – she studied
sculpture – and this is reflected in the way she works, preferring to
paint her designs in watercolour before transferring them onto fabric
and stitching freehand. Her cross-stitch designs have been published in
magazines for over ten years. As well as her magazine work, Leslie
has written two previous books, *The Snowman in Cross Stitch,* and her
most recent book, published by GMC Publications in 2004,
Paddington Bear in Cross Stitch. She likes to spend time in the
countryside, fishing and painting.

Index

Bolder type indicates the title of a project

A

AIDA 14
Anchor threads 14
'As good as his mother ever made!' 79–81
Attwell, Emily 23
Attwell, Augustus 23
Attwell, Mabel Lucie 23, 27, 33, 37, 41, 45, 49, 53, 57, 65, 69, 79, 87, 91, 95, 105, 109, 113, 117, 121
Attwell, Norman 37
Auntie's bathing suit 45–7

B

back stitch 16
bathroom accessories 95–9
bathroom plaque: **'Please remember'** 83–5
blanket stitch 17
Blowing a kiss 41–3
'Boo-Boo' stationery 73–7
bookmark 76
bootees 30
Boy with dog 121–3

'The bride, God bless her. The bridegroom, God help him' 37–9
buttonhole stitch 17

C

Chambers, W & R 33
Charles, Prince 109
colour of threads 14
count of fabrics 14
cross stitching 15
cushion 105–7

D

Daily Sketch 65
DMC threads 14
door plate 113–15

E

Earnshaw, Brian ('Bill') 65, 91
Earnshaw, Harold ('Pat') 33, 37, 61, 91, 101
Earnshaw, Max ('Peter') 53
enlarging charts 14

F

fabrics 14–15
The fisherman 101–3

MABEL LUCIE ATTWELL

'Forget-me-not' 91–3
frames, using 17

G

'Get well quickly!' 33–5
Girl with dog 61–3
Good luck 69–71

H

half cross stitch 16
Hamblett, Charles 65
hand towel 96–7

Hills, Leslie Norah 125
Homes and Gardens 117
hoops, using 18

I

'I likes 'oo' 109–11

J

'Just a bundle of love' 49–51

K

knots 18

L

label 77
layette 27–31
locating first stitch
    15

M

materials 14–15
metallic threads 14
mitring corners 19
mounting
    embroidery 19

N

needles 14
note block 73–5

P

Peeping Pansy 69
photocopying charts
    14
'Please remember'
    bathroom plaque
    83–5
'Puppy' cushion
    105–7

Q

*Queen's Book of the
    Red Cross* 113

R

*Raphael House
    Library of Gift
    Books* 49

rattle 31
Romania, Queen of
    69, 79

S

Secrets 87–9
Sitting by the fire
    53–5
slate frames 17
soap dispenser 98–9
St Martin's School
    of Art 33
stitches
    back stitch 16
    blanket (buttonhole)
        stitch 17
    cross stitching 15
    half cross stitch 16
    locating first 15
    three-quarter stitch
        16
unpicking 18
suppliers 124

T

techniques 15–19
**'They finks I'se
    going to sleep!'**
    65–7
**'This one's for you,
    dear'** 23–5
threads 14
knots in 18
three-quarter stitch 16
tooth mug 98–9

U

unpicking work 18
'UR A1 UR!' 57–9

V

Valentine & Sons 57
vest, baby's 28–9

W

washing method
    18–19

'White rabbits'
    117–19
Wickham, Marjorie
    ('Peggy') (née
    Earnshaw) 41,
    49, 87, 95, 113,
    121
Wickham, Michael
    87

GMC Publications,
Castle Place, 166 High Street, Lewes, East Sussex BN7 1XU United Kingdom
Tel: 01273 488005 Fax: 01273 402866
E-mail: pubs@thegmcgroup.com
Website: www.gmcbooks.com

Contact us for a complete catalogue, or visit our website.
Orders by credit card are accepted.